30-DAY GOAL TASK TRACKER

Copyright © 2022 by Katie Nelson

All rights reserved. No part of this book may be reproduced in any form without written permission from the author or publisher, except as permitted by law.

DoBetterBeMore.com

ISBN: 979-8-9871203-0-9

Printed in the United States of America

Introduction

We all could use some daily guidance to help us reach our goals. This tracker is intended to help us focus on our daily tasks that have to be completed in order to achieve our goal.

If this tracker is used properly, it can be a gauge of how well you perform each day when it comes to working towards your personal goal.

Take the time to fill out each page in the morning and review your day every night. Learn from your day so that you can do better the next day.

Every 7 days you are going to review your past week and write down your wins and losses. Then you are going to write out your biggest success for that week.

At the end of the 30 days, you are going to review the entire month, tally all the days you succeeded, all the days you failed and write them down on the summary sheet at the end.

Review your losses, summarize how you are going to *do better* and set your next goal so you can *be more*.

Do Better every day, even if is just 1% better, and you will always *Be More*!

I AM COMMITTED

DO BETTER

BE MORE

Instructions

Let's start with where you want to be in 30 days.

30-day goal:

_____

_____

What are you doing now that is preventing you from achieving this goal? Are you willing to give it up?

_____

_____

What steps are you going to do every day that will direct you to your goal? (Pick 5)

_____

_____

_____

_____

_____

Don't wait until Monday, next week, first of the month, or the first of the year... **START TODAY**.

Fill out each page daily review the day's wins and losses.

This is for you, and you alone!!

If you do not complete all 5 tasks for the day, reflect on how you are going to *DO BETTER* the next day and carry on.

IT'S TIME FOR YOU TO *BE MORE*

I AM COMMITTED

DO BETTER   BE MORE

I AM COMMITTED

DO BETTER   BE MORE

Date: ___ / ___   Day 1.

30-Day Goal: _____

TASK 1: _____
TASK 2: _____
TASK 3: _____
TASK 4: _____
TASK 5: _____

TODAY'S WINS:

_____
_____
_____

TODAY'S LOSES:

_____
_____
_____

HOW AM I GOING TO DO BETTER TOMORROW:

_____
_____
_____

I AM COMMITTED

DO BETTER   BE MORE

Date: ___ / ___   Day 2.

30-Day Goal: _____

☐ TASK 1: _____
☐ TASK 2: _____
☐ TASK 3: _____
☐ TASK 4: _____
☐ TASK 5: _____

TODAY'S WINS:

_____
_____
_____

TODAY'S LOSES:

_____
_____
_____

HOW AM I GOING TO DO BETTER TOMORROW:

_____
_____
_____

I AM COMMITTED

DO BETTER   BE MORE

Date: ___ / ___   Day 3.

30-Day Goal: _____

] TASK 1: _____

] TASK 2: _____

] TASK 3: _____

] TASK 4: _____

] TASK 5: _____

TODAY'S WINS:

_____

_____

_____

TODAY'S LOSES:

_____

_____

_____

HOW AM I GOING TO DO BETTER TOMORROW:

_____

_____

_____

I AM COMMITTED

DO BETTER   BE MORE

Date: ___ / ___   Day 4.

30-Day Goal: _____

- ☐ TASK 1: _____
- ☐ TASK 2: _____
- ☐ TASK 3: _____
- ☐ TASK 4: _____
- ☐ TASK 5: _____

TODAY'S WINS:

_____
_____
_____

TODAY'S LOSES:

_____
_____
_____

HOW AM I GOING TO DO BETTER TOMORROW:

_____
_____
_____

I AM COMMITTED

DO BETTER   BE MORE

Date: ___ / ___   Day 5.

30-Day Goal: _____

TASK 1: _____
TASK 2: _____
TASK 3: _____
TASK 4: _____
TASK 5: _____

TODAY'S WINS:

_____

_____

_____

TODAY'S LOSES:

_____

_____

_____

HOW AM I GOING TO DO BETTER TOMORROW:

_____

_____

_____

I AM COMMITTED

DO BETTER   BE MORE

Date: ___ / ___　　　　　Day 6.

30-Day Goal: _____

- ☐ TASK 1: _____
- ☐ TASK 2: _____
- ☐ TASK 3: _____
- ☐ TASK 4: _____
- ☐ TASK 5: _____

TODAY'S WINS:

_____

_____

_____

TODAY'S LOSES:

_____

_____

_____

HOW AM I GOING TO DO BETTER TOMORROW:

_____

_____

_____

I AM COMMITTED

DO BETTER　　　　　　　　　　　　　　　　　　　　BE MORE

Date: ___ / ___   Day 7.

30-Day Goal: _____

TASK 1: _____
TASK 2: _____
TASK 3: _____
TASK 4: _____
TASK 5: _____

TODAY'S WINS:

_____
_____
_____

TODAY'S LOSES:

_____
_____
_____

HOW AM I GOING TO DO BETTER TOMORROW:

_____
_____
_____

I AM COMMITTED

DO BETTER   BE MORE

7 Day Recap

Wins:

- ☐ _____
- ☐ _____
- ☐ _____
- ☐ _____
- ☐ _____
- ☐ _____

Lessons Learned:

- ☐ _____
- ☐ _____
- ☐ _____
- ☐ _____
- ☐ _____
- ☐ _____

This week's success story:

_____

_____

I AM COMMITTED

DO BETTER   BE MORE

Date: ___ / ___   Day 8.

30-Day Goal: _____

] TASK 1: _____
] TASK 2: _____
] TASK 3: _____
] TASK 4: _____
] TASK 5: _____

TODAY'S WINS:

_____
_____
_____

TODAY'S LOSES:

_____
_____
_____

HOW AM I GOING TO DO BETTER TOMORROW:

_____
_____
_____

I AM COMMITTED
DO BETTER   BE MORE

Date: ___ / ___   Day 9.

30-Day Goal: _____

- ☐ TASK 1: _____
- ☐ TASK 2: _____
- ☐ TASK 3: _____
- ☐ TASK 4: _____
- ☐ TASK 5: _____

TODAY'S WINS:

_____

_____

_____

TODAY'S LOSES:

_____

_____

_____

HOW AM I GOING TO DO BETTER TOMORROW:

_____

_____

_____

I AM COMMITTED

DO BETTER   BE MORE

Date: ___ / ___   Day 10.

30-Day Goal: _____

TASK 1: _____

TASK 2: _____

TASK 3: _____

TASK 4: _____

TASK 5: _____

TODAY'S WINS:

_____

_____

_____

TODAY'S LOSES:

_____

_____

_____

HOW AM I GOING TO DO BETTER TOMORROW:

_____

_____

_____

I AM COMMITTED

DO BETTER   BE MORE

Date: ___ / ___   Day 11.

30-Day Goal: _____

- [ ] TASK 1: _____
- [ ] TASK 2: _____
- [ ] TASK 3: _____
- [ ] TASK 4: _____
- [ ] TASK 5: _____

TODAY'S WINS:

_____

_____

_____

TODAY'S LOSES:

_____

_____

_____

HOW AM I GOING TO DO BETTER TOMORROW:

_____

_____

_____

I AM COMMITTED

DO BETTER   BE MORE

Date: ___ / ___   Day 12.

30-Day Goal: _____

TASK 1: _____
TASK 2: _____
TASK 3: _____
TASK 4: _____
TASK 5: _____

TODAY'S WINS:

_____
_____
_____

TODAY'S LOSES:

_____
_____
_____

HOW AM I GOING TO DO BETTER TOMORROW:

_____
_____
_____

I AM COMMITTED

DO BETTER   BE MORE

Date: ___ / ___   Day 13.

30-Day Goal: _____

- ☐ TASK 1: _____
- ☐ TASK 2: _____
- ☐ TASK 3: _____
- ☐ TASK 4: _____
- ☐ TASK 5: _____

TODAY'S WINS:

_____

_____

_____

TODAY'S LOSES:

_____

_____

_____

HOW AM I GOING TO DO BETTER TOMORROW:

_____

_____

_____

I AM COMMITTED

DO BETTER   BE MORE

Date: ___ / ___   Day 14.

30-Day Goal: _____

] TASK 1: _____

] TASK 2: _____

] TASK 3: _____

] TASK 4: _____

] TASK 5: _____

TODAY'S WINS:

_____

_____

_____

TODAY'S LOSES:

_____

_____

_____

HOW AM I GOING TO DO BETTER TOMORROW:

_____

_____

_____

I AM COMMITTED

DO BETTER   BE MORE

7 Day Recap

Wins:

- [ ] _____
- [ ] _____
- [ ] _____
- [ ] _____
- [ ] _____
- [ ] _____
- [ ] _____

Lessons Learned:

- [ ] _____
- [ ] _____
- [ ] _____
- [ ] _____
- [ ] _____
- [ ] _____

This week's success story:

_____

_____

I AM COMMITTED

DO BETTER					BE MORE

Date: ___ / ___ Day 15.

30-Day Goal: _____

TASK 1: _____

TASK 2: _____

TASK 3: _____

TASK 4: _____

TASK 5: _____

TODAY'S WINS:

_____

_____

_____

TODAY'S LOSES:

_____

_____

_____

HOW AM I GOING TO DO BETTER TOMORROW:

_____

_____

_____

I AM COMMITTED

DO BETTER   BE MORE

Date: ___ / ___   Day 16.

30-Day Goal: _____

☐ TASK 1: _____
☐ TASK 2: _____
☐ TASK 3: _____
☐ TASK 4: _____
☐ TASK 5: _____

TODAY'S WINS:

_____
_____
_____

TODAY'S LOSES:

_____
_____
_____

HOW AM I GOING TO DO BETTER TOMORROW:

_____
_____
_____

I AM COMMITTED

DO BETTER   BE MORE

Date: ___ / ___   Day 17.

30-Day Goal: _____

TASK 1: _____
TASK 2: _____
TASK 3: _____
TASK 4: _____
TASK 5: _____

TODAY'S WINS:

_____
_____
_____

TODAY'S LOSES:

_____
_____
_____

HOW AM I GOING TO DO BETTER TOMORROW:

_____
_____
_____

I AM COMMITTED

DO BETTER   BE MORE

Date: ___ / ___   Day 18.

30-Day Goal: _____

- ☐ TASK 1: _____
- ☐ TASK 2: _____
- ☐ TASK 3: _____
- ☐ TASK 4: _____
- ☐ TASK 5: _____

TODAY'S WINS:

_____

_____

_____

TODAY'S LOSES:

_____

_____

_____

HOW AM I GOING TO DO BETTER TOMORROW:

_____

_____

_____

I AM COMMITTED

DO BETTER   BE MORE

Date: ___ / ___   Day 19.

30-Day Goal: _____

] TASK 1: _____

] TASK 2: _____

] TASK 3: _____

] TASK 4: _____

] TASK 5: _____

TODAY'S WINS:

_____

_____

_____

TODAY'S LOSES:

_____

_____

_____

HOW AM I GOING TO DO BETTER TOMORROW:

_____

_____

_____

I AM COMMITTED

DO BETTER   BE MORE

Date: ___ / ___   Day 20.

30-Day Goal: _____

- ☐ TASK 1: _____
- ☐ TASK 2: _____
- ☐ TASK 3: _____
- ☐ TASK 4: _____
- ☐ TASK 5: _____

TODAY'S WINS:

_____

_____

_____

TODAY'S LOSES:

_____

_____

_____

HOW AM I GOING TO DO BETTER TOMORROW:

_____

_____

_____

I AM COMMITTED

DO BETTER   BE MORE

Date: ___ / ___   Day 21.

30-Day Goal: _____

TASK 1: _____

TASK 2: _____

TASK 3: _____

TASK 4: _____

TASK 5: _____

TODAY'S WINS:

_____

_____

_____

TODAY'S LOSES:

_____

_____

_____

HOW AM I GOING TO DO BETTER TOMORROW:

_____

_____

_____

I AM COMMITTED

DO BETTER   BE MORE

7 Day Recap

Wins:

- [ ] _____
- [ ] _____
- [ ] _____
- [ ] _____
- [ ] _____
- [ ] _____
- [ ] _____

Lessons Learned:

- [ ] _____
- [ ] _____
- [ ] _____
- [ ] _____
- [ ] _____
- [ ] _____

This week's success story:

_____

_____

I AM COMMITTED

DO BETTER   BE MORE

Date: ___ / ___   Day 22.

30-Day Goal: _____

TASK 1: _____
TASK 2: _____
TASK 3: _____
TASK 4: _____
TASK 5: _____

TODAY'S WINS:

_____
_____
_____

TODAY'S LOSES:

_____
_____
_____

HOW AM I GOING TO DO BETTER TOMORROW:

_____
_____
_____

I AM COMMITTED

DO BETTER   BE MORE

Date: ___ / ___   Day 23.

30-Day Goal: _____

- ☐ TASK 1: _____
- ☐ TASK 2: _____
- ☐ TASK 3: _____
- ☐ TASK 4: _____
- ☐ TASK 5: _____

TODAY'S WINS:

_____

_____

_____

TODAY'S LOSES:

_____

_____

_____

HOW AM I GOING TO DO BETTER TOMORROW:

_____

_____

_____

I AM COMMITTED

DO BETTER   BE MORE

Date: ___ /___   Day 24.

30-Day Goal: _____

] TASK 1: _____

] TASK 2: _____

] TASK 3: _____

] TASK 4: _____

] TASK 5: _____

TODAY'S WINS:

_____

_____

_____

TODAY'S LOSES:

_____

_____

_____

HOW AM I GOING TO DO BETTER TOMORROW:

_____

_____

_____

I AM COMMITTED

DO BETTER   BE MORE

Date: ___ / ___   Day 25.

30-Day Goal: _____

- [ ] TASK 1: _____
- [ ] TASK 2: _____
- [ ] TASK 3: _____
- [ ] TASK 4: _____
- [ ] TASK 5: _____

TODAY'S WINS:

_____

_____

_____

TODAY'S LOSES:

_____

_____

_____

HOW AM I GOING TO DO BETTER TOMORROW:

_____

_____

_____

I AM COMMITTED

DO BETTER   BE MORE

Date: ___ / ___ Day 26.

30-Day Goal: _____

TASK 1: _____
TASK 2: _____
TASK 3: _____
TASK 4: _____
TASK 5: _____

TODAY'S WINS:

_____
_____
_____

TODAY'S LOSES:

_____
_____
_____

HOW AM I GOING TO DO BETTER TOMORROW:

_____
_____
_____

I AM COMMITTED

DO BETTER   BE MORE

Date: ___ / ___   Day 27.

30-Day Goal: _____

- [ ] TASK 1: _____
- [ ] TASK 2: _____
- [ ] TASK 3: _____
- [ ] TASK 4: _____
- [ ] TASK 5: _____

TODAY'S WINS:

_____

_____

_____

TODAY'S LOSES:

_____

_____

_____

HOW AM I GOING TO DO BETTER TOMORROW:

_____

_____

_____

I AM COMMITTED

DO BETTER   BE MORE

Date: ___ / ___   Day 28.

30-Day Goal: _____

TASK 1: _____
TASK 2: _____
TASK 3: _____
TASK 4: _____
TASK 5: _____

TODAY'S WINS:

_____
_____
_____

TODAY'S LOSES:

_____
_____
_____

HOW AM I GOING TO DO BETTER TOMORROW:

_____
_____
_____

I AM COMMITTED

DO BETTER   BE MORE

Date: ___ / ___   Day 29.

30-Day Goal: _____

☐ TASK 1: _____
☐ TASK 2: _____
☐ TASK 3: _____
☐ TASK 4: _____
☐ TASK 5: _____

TODAY'S WINS:

_____
_____
_____

TODAY'S LOSES:

_____
_____
_____

HOW AM I GOING TO DO BETTER TOMORROW:

_____
_____
_____

I AM COMMITTED

DO BETTER   BE MORE

Date: ___ / ___   Day 30.

30-Day Goal: _____

] TASK 1: _____

] TASK 2: _____

] TASK 3: _____

] TASK 4: _____

] TASK 5: _____

TODAY'S WINS:

_____

_____

_____

TODAY'S LOSES:

_____

_____

_____

HOW AM I GOING TO DO BETTER TOMORROW:

_____

_____

_____

I AM COMMITTED

DO BETTER   BE MORE

30-Day Recap

Did you Reach your 30-Day goal: YES / NO

How are you going to improve going forward:

_____

_____

_____

_____

Time to start your next success story.

What is your next 30-Day Goal?

_____

_____

_____

Follow the link below to order more Success Essentials:

DoBetterBeMore.com

Share your Success:

#dobetterbemore

I AM COMMITTED

DO BETTER   BE MORE

Notes:

I AM COMMITTED

DO BETTER   BE MORE

Notes:

DO BETTER I AM COMMITTED BE MORE

Notes:

I AM COMMITTED

DO BETTER   BE MORE

Notes:

DO BETTER I AM COMMITTED BE MORE

Notes:

DO BETTER **I AM COMMITTED** BE MORE

www.ingramcontent.com/pod-product-compliance
Lightning Source LLC
Chambersburg PA
CBHW051351040426
42453CB00007B/510